AESOP'S FABLES

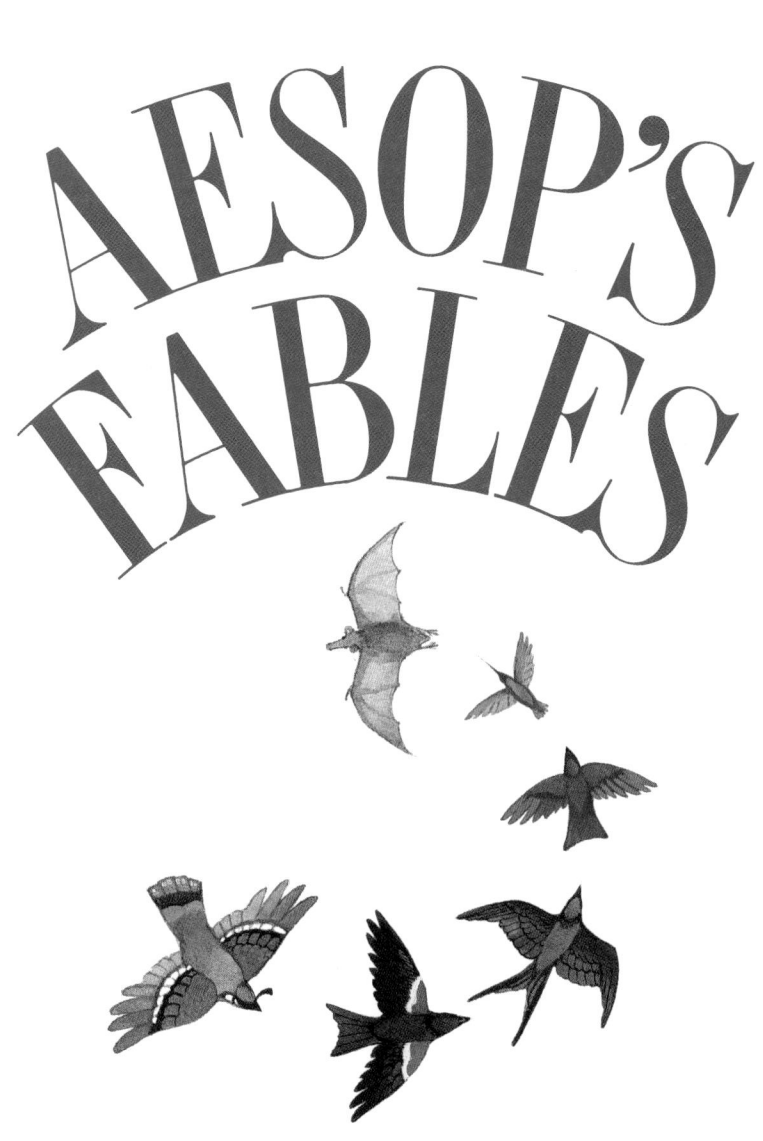

Retold by Susan Cornell Poskanzer
Pictures by Delana Bettoli

Silver Press

for my Grandfather Rudy
my father Phillip
and Autumn in Silverton
—D.B.

Library of Congress Cataloging-in-Publication Data

Poskanzer, Susan Cornell.
Aesop's fables / retold by Susan Cornell Poskanzer, pictures by Delana Bettoli.
p. cm.
Summary: An illustrated collection of thirty fables retold from Aesop, including
"Androcles and the Lion," "The City Mouse and the Country Mouse,"
and "The Wolf in Sheep's Clothing."
1. Fables. [1. Fables.] I. Bettoli, Delana, ill. II. Title.
PZ8.2.P56Ae 1992
398.2′452—dc20
[E]
90-26465
CIP
AC
ISBN 0-671-74116-0
ISBN 0-671-74117-9 LSB

Text copyright © 1992 Silver Press

Illustration copyright © 1992 Delana Bettoli

Published by Silver Press, a division of Silver Burdett Press, Inc.,
Simon & Schuster, Inc., Prentice Hall Bldg., Englewood Cliffs, NJ 07632.

Printed in the United States of America.

Designed by Virginia Pope-Boehling
Art Directed by Linda Huber

10 9 8 7 6 5 4 3 2 1

Contents

Androcles and the Lion

Long ago, a slave named Androcles worked for a cruel master. One day, unable to stand this harsh life any longer, Androcles ran away. Racing through a thick forest, he heard crying and moaning.

"A lion!" exclaimed Androcles, seeing a huge beast stretched on the ground. "He could tear my head off in one blow!"

Androcles shook with fear, but he had a kind heart, and couldn't bear to leave without finding out why the lion was crying.

"Show me what is wrong," Androcles whispered gently.

The lion lifted a swollen paw with a sharp thorn stuck right in the middle. Forgetting his fear, Androcles gently removed the thorn, and washed the wound with cool stream water. He nursed the lion for weeks until one day Roman soldiers discovered the pair in the woods and dragged them away.

Androcles was found guilty of running away from his master. As punishment, he would have to fight a ferocious lion in the great arena of Rome.

On the terrible day, everyone, including the emperor, came to see Androcles fight the lion. Androcles waited in the center of the arena, holding his breath, as soldiers unlatched the cage of a tremendous, very hungry lion.

At once, the starving lion raced to attack. But just as the beast leaped to tear Androcles apart, it stopped and looked into his eyes. Then, with the whole city watching, the lion gently licked the slave's face, like a playful kitten. This was, of course, the lion Androcles had saved. The Roman emperor was so impressed that he freed Androcles and the lion.

Androcles was grateful that:

A Kind Soul Never Forgets a Kind Deed.

The Beekeeper

One hot, hazy afternoon the hives in a bee garden were quiet. Most of the bees were out gathering sweet nectar from the wildflowers, while the beekeeper was at market selling jars of thick honey.

Suddenly, a honey robber darted into the garden. He peeked into the bee houses, then pressed his ear to the hives.

"It's quiet!" he chuckled. "Just as I hoped."

Using a flat stick, he scraped fine honey into a fat clay jar.

"Delicious!" he said, sucking honey from his fingers.

In less than ten minutes, the hives were cleaned out. Then the honey robber ran from the garden.

Soon bees buzzed home from the fields, their legs covered with sweet wildflower nectar. They strained toward the hives with their heavy loads.

"It's all gone!" they buzzed when they saw the stripped hives. "The beekeeper always used to leave enough for us. How could she do this!"

Swarms of angry bees buzzed around the hives.

Meanwhile, the tired beekeeper trudged home from the market.

"I can't wait to see my lovely bees," she hummed, strolling into the garden.

But the beekeeper didn't get far. When the bees saw her, hundreds of them covered her body. Furiously, they stung hard, leaving large red bumps. Then they followed their queen and moved far away to build new lives in new hives.

Swollen and angry, the beekeeper was left alone, wishing her bees had learned one important lesson:

Be Sure You Know Your Friends from Your Enemies.

The Birds, the Beasts, and the Bat

The birds and the beasts had waged a terrible war for years. No one remembered how the fighting started, but everyone was angry. Bat didn't want to end up losing anything. So she promised both sides she would consider helping them in the war.

"Join us," yelled the birds. "You fly and we fly. You surely belong with us!" they argued.

"No, you belong with us," pleaded the lions, tigers, and other beasts. "You have fur and we have fur. Join us," they begged.

But Bat stayed to herself and joined no one. Then, just when it seemed certain that the beasts would win the long war, Bat joined their side.

"It's a little late," grumbled the beasts, and never thought much of Bat again. Bat paid no attention.

"Ha!" she cried. "Now I'm on the side of the winners and will gain the prizes of war."

But war is strange, and unexpected things happen. Just one day later, the birds won the long, terrible war.

"So you joined the beasts after all," screeched the birds into Bat's ears.

"Well, just for a short time," Bat explained, trying to worm her way out of the situation.

But the birds would not forgive her. They made her live in darkness forever after. From then on, Bat flew through damp and dark caves, knowing it is wise to:

Choose Sides for What You Believe in, Not for What You Might Win.

The Boy and the Wolf

Out in a grassy field, a shepherd boy tended his family's sheep.

"I'm hot," he moaned. "And it's so boring out here alone with these dreary sheep."

Suddenly, an idea sparked into his head.

"Wolf! Wolf!" he screamed until his face was red.

The boy's family raced to the fields with weapons, for one wolf could destroy the whole flock of sheep and ruin them.

"Where is the wolf?" they shouted to the boy.

"There is no wolf," laughed the boy. "I was just lonely and thought we needed some excitement."

"Silly boy," scolded the boy's mother. "We work hard and have no time for pranks. You must never fool us again."

The next morning, the boy thought, "How quickly they came! How exciting it was!"

The boy could not resist.

"Wolf! Wolf!" he screamed again.

Once again, his family scurried up the hill.

"Where? Where?" roared the boy's father.

You can just imagine what his family said when they learned the boy had tricked them again.

Later that afternoon, a hungry gray wolf crept across the field as the boy was yawning.

"Help!" yelled the startled boy. "REALLY! WOLF!"

No one appeared. The boy's family heard his screams, but just grumbled loudly. The wolf could hardly believe his good luck, and enjoyed a magnificent dinner of four sheep and a lamb.

Later, these words echoed all over town:

"If People Think You Are a Liar, No One Will Ever Believe You."

The City Mouse
and the Country Mouse

Country Mouse invited his cousin, City Mouse, for a day in the country. To prepare for the visit, Country Mouse collected roots, stale bread crusts, and moldy cheese rinds.

"So glad you've come," said Country Mouse graciously when his cousin arrived.

"So nice of you to invite me," answered City Mouse.

Country Mouse proudly showed City Mouse to his nest where he'd set out the food. Starting to chew a stale crust of bread, Country Mouse realized City Mouse was snickering.

"Really, Cousin," laughed City Mouse. "How can you live on old roots, stale bread, and moldy cheese? You really must come to the city to see how splendid life can be."

"Life in the country may be plain, but it's peaceful," said Country Mouse, suddenly feeling terribly poor. "But if you wish, I'll go to see your home."

So they left for the city. Scampering into his cousin's elegant town house, Country Mouse was instantly impressed. A magnificent dinner lay on crisp white linen on the dining room table, for there had been a party that night.

"Please help yourself," said City Mouse.

For the first time in his life, Country Mouse feasted on fresh bread, ripe cheeses, and rich puddings. But then three people and two huge dogs suddenly entered the great dining room. Immediately, the dogs raced for the mice. City Mouse and Country Mouse felt hot breath on their tails as they escaped into a small hole under a windowsill.

Country Mouse's heart thumped wildly. If he hadn't been gasping for air, he would have said:

"It Is Better to Eat Plain Food in Peace than to Feast in Fear."

The Crow and the Pitcher

One hot morning, Crow's throat felt dry and scratchy as sand as he flew over the countryside.

"I'm so thirsty," he cawed, searching for water.

Lucky for Crow, he spotted a tall, rusty pitcher in a stony field. Instantly, Crow glided in for a smooth landing right on top of the pitcher. Poking one eye over the opening, Crow was delighted to see water at the bottom. He dipped his beak into the pitcher, but found he was way short of a drink.

"I can't reach the water!" he screeched. "My beak is too short, and the pitcher is too tall."

He jumped off the pitcher and looked at it from every angle. Finally, an idea flew into his head.

"I'll push the pitcher over!" he exclaimed. "When the pitcher hits the stones on the ground, it will crack and splinter. Then I'll drink the water as it runs over the ground."

But then Crow thought again.

"No, no," he moaned. "I'll get only a tiny bit of the water that way. Most of it will trickle out and be lost to the field."

Once again, Crow stepped back from the pitcher. He hopped around, then looked into it.

"Ah ha!" he cawed. "How clever I am!"

With his beak, Crow picked up a little stone in the field and dropped it into the pitcher. Soon he found another, and then another. As Crow's pebbles plinked one by one into the pitcher's narrow opening, the water rose higher and higher until it reached the brim.

"How refreshing!" said Crow, dipping his beak into the cool water. "If I hadn't been so thirsty, I wouldn't have figured out the solution."

In other words:

Where There's a Will, There's a Way.

The Crow in Peacock Feathers

C row perched on a lovely stone garden wall. Inside the wall were water fountains, carved bushes, wide lawns, scarlet flowers, and a pair of handsome peacocks.

"Look how they strut in their magnificent colors!" Crow thought.

He saw every shade of blue, green, and yellow in their bright feathers. Looking at his own black feathers, he felt plain and poor.

"If only I had fancy feathers," he moaned.

Then he noticed shimmering peacock feathers on the lawn near the carved bushes.

"They will suit me well!" he chuckled.

Crow gathered the peacock feathers and stuck them into his own. He pranced around the garden, feeling grand.

"Who do you think YOU are?" asked the peacocks, laughing at Crow in his borrowed feathers. "Those feathers don't belong to you. You look quite ridiculous."

Then the peacocks pecked away until they had plucked all the colorful feathers from silly Crow. In fact, they were so rough that Crow lost quite a few feathers of his own, too. Naked, Crow flew back over the garden wall.

He joined the other crows, and the sparrows, starlings, and pigeons. But they would have nothing to do with him.

"We saw you in the peacock's garden wearing fancy feathers," they said. "Surely, we're not grand enough company for the likes of you."

They flew off, leaving poor crow bald, alone, and thinking:

Fancy Feathers Don't Make Fancy Birds.

The Dog and His Shadow

Dog's mouth watered as he looked through the butcher shop window. It just happened that at that moment the butcher's young daughter was glancing outside.

"Look at that sweet dog," the little girl said. "He looks so hungry. Daddy, please may I give him something?"

To please his daughter, the butcher chose a thick beef bone. The little girl opened the shop door and gave Dog the fine bone. Dog smiled and pranced proudly down the street.

"Surely, this is the biggest bone in the county," thought Dog. "Won't my friends be jealous when they see what I've got!"

But on the way home, Dog crossed a wooden bridge over a quiet brook. He looked down into the water and was more than surprised.

"There's a dog down there," he thought. "How cocky he is! Look at the size of that bone in his mouth. It's even bigger than mine!"

Dog was staring at a reflection of himself, but he didn't know this. He growled. The other dog growled right back. Dog could take no more.

"What makes you think you're so fine? Why should your bone be even bigger than mine?" he barked fiercely.

When Dog spoke, his bone fell right out of his mouth and splashed into the water.

"My prize bone!" screamed Dog, and jumped off the bridge into the brook.

He swam, looking for his bone for hours, but never found it. Poor Dog! He didn't know what you know:

If You Are Not Grateful for What You Have, You May Lose It.

The Fisherman's Good Luck

Early on a gray, foggy morning, a fisherman untied his boat from the dock. He rowed to his favorite spot in the river and baited his lines with tiny silver minnows.

"Morning is the best time to catch fish," he said.

The fisherman kept his eyes on the lines, watching for the sharp snap of a fish. But the lines were still, and no fish was tempted by the shiny silver bait.

Soon the sun came out and blazed overhead. The fisherman ate a sardine sandwich he'd packed in his tackle box. Then he washed down his lunch with cider.

"What miserable luck!" he grumbled. "No bites at all. But if I'm patient, maybe the fish will start to nibble."

Afternoon breezes blew gently over the green water. The fisherman leaned over the side of the boat, searching for fish.

"Only weeds and snails right now," he mumbled, "but no doubt the fish will soon arrive."

Later, as the sun glowed orange in the sky, the fisherman grew warm and restless in the rocking boat.

"Come on, fish. Bite! It's not too late," he sang to the invisible fish beneath his boat.

But soon it was dusk and time to row to shore. The fisherman was ready to reel in his lines and pack up his tackle. But he hated to go home empty-handed.

"I've stayed all day. What's two more minutes to me? I'll wait just a bit longer," he whispered.

At that very instant, a giant fish rose from the river. It flew through the air and landed right in the fisherman's lap.

"What a fine surprise!" said the lucky man, smiling into the fish's face.

The fisherman knew:

Patience Is Rewarded.

The Fox and the Crow

Crow perched high in an oak tree. She held in her beak a thick piece of sharp cheese stolen from a kitchen windowsill. Fox's nose twitched as he passed Crow's tree.

"Ah, someone nearby has a fragrant bit of cheese," he said, catching the scent from high in the tree. "Perhaps I can steal it away."

Fox looked up. Light flickered through the umbrella of oak leaves on Crow's tree. In the shadows, Fox saw Crow was about to eat the fine cheese.

"Hello, Miss Crow," Fox said sweetly. "What a sight you are up there! You must be the most handsome bird in the entire woods."

"This sly fox must take me for a fool," Crow thought. "If I answer, he will snatch the cheese as soon as I open my mouth."

After a few minutes, Fox realized Crow was not about to fall for his trick. So he gathered his wits and tried again.

"Dear Crow," Fox sang, "I've heard you have a most wonderful voice. If your song does indeed match your splendid looks, then truly, you are the finest bird in the woods!"

Now Crow listened carefully. She'd been told that her caw was far from beautiful, so it was happy news indeed if Fox thought otherwise.

Fox saw her interest and continued, "Crow, let me hear just a bit of your sweet song. Then I'll know all I heard is true."

These words so greatly flattered Crow that she opened her mouth to sing for Fox. Of course, the cheese fell to the ground, and Fox promptly snatched it up. Instead of lunch, Crow was left with an important lesson:

Never Trust a Flatterer.

The Fox and the Grapes

Fox napped soundly on a warm summer day. Hot and thirsty, he dreamed of having a cool, refreshing snack. When he awoke, he saw bunches of purple grapes, hanging from an arbor above him.

"How juicy they look!" Fox exclaimed.

He stood up to pick a plump bunch of grapes, only to find that he couldn't reach it.

"I'll stand on that rock," he said, pushing a heavy stone under the arbor. "Then I'll pluck those grapes and have a fine feast."

This time he was just inches short of reaching the fat bunches of grapes. Fox was hungrier and thirstier than ever.

"Those grapes look so juicy and delicious," said Fox. "I'll scream if I can't have some."

With those words, Fox lunged at the arbor, jumping higher than ever. But he succeeded only in falling on his head, far from the grapes.

Then, from the opposite direction, he leaped high in the air, aiming for a different bunch of grapes. But once again, he landed empty-handed. Fox's mouth watered at the thought of eating the ripe grapes. Bubbles of sweat formed on his forehead.

"I'll jump even higher," he said, springing into the air once again for the grapes.

But it wasn't high enough, and Fox only slapped at the juicy prize. Finally, Fox shook his head.

"I don't think I want that fruit after all," he said. "It's probably moldy and full of worms anyway."

With that, Fox walked away, never realizing:

It Is Easy to Say You Don't Want What You Can't Have.

The Frog and the Ox

Two young frogs were playing in a stream when they came upon a beast bigger than anything they'd ever seen. In fright, they raced home downstream to report their amazing experience.

"Mother!" they screamed. "You will never believe what we just saw. It was a huge monster with two wicked horns, hooves , and a long, long tail."

"Ha!" laughed their mother. "That was only the ox. True, it is large, but with just a little effort, I can make myself just as big as the ox. Just watch."

Mother Frog puffed herself up and proudly asked, "I'm as big as the ox right now, aren't I?"

"No, Mother, it was far bigger than that," they answered.

So their mother took a deep breath and puffed herself to twice the size as before.

"Am I as big as the ox now?" she groaned.

"Oh, no, no," exclaimed the two small frogs. "The ox was ever so much bigger than that."

Now she took an even deeper breath and concentrated very, very hard before she blew herself up bigger than she had ever been before.

"Surely, this must be as big as the ox," she moaned, almost bursting.

"No," screamed the excited little frogs. "It was even bigger."

So poor Mother Frog took an absolutely enormous breath and puffed, and puffed herself up until she simply burst. POP!

Too bad she didn't understand that:

It Is Impossible to Do the Impossible.

The Gnat and the Bull

Fat, old Bull was grazing in a muddy field as tiny Gnat buzzed around the puddles at his feet. After a while, Gnat flew up and discovered Bull's horns. She flew around and around them until at last she landed on Bull's left horn, and was silent for a few moments.

"I've been resting here for a while," she thought. "Perhaps I should shift my weight so Bull will not get tired."

Gnat leaned the other way as Bull continued grazing. Then Gnat continued thinking.

"I see there is another horn on the other side of this bull," said Gnat to herself. "I will fly there and rest for a while, for it is inconsiderate of me to stay too long on one horn."

Gnat flew to the other horn while Bull finished eating his dinner. But the insect was uneasy, and now she spoke to Bull.

"Excuse me, please," said Gnat sweetly. "But you are such a kind host, and I have no wish to overstay my welcome. If at any time I feel too heavy for you, let me know. I will gladly fly away and come back after you've rested. Believe me, I don't want to burden you, so just let me know when I tire you in any way."

Bull chewed the last of the sweet grass, blinked, and said, "It makes no difference to me if you stay or go. Honestly, I didn't even know you were there until you spoke."

Gnat was surprised, but the tiny bug had learned something new:

Don't Fool Yourself into Thinking You're More Important than You Are.

The Goose that Laid the Golden Eggs

A poor farmer named Fred rose early to gather eggs from his geese, as he did every day. Reaching under a plain gray goose, he saw something bright and shiny.

"What do we have here?" Fred asked the bird.

Then he saw an egg unlike any he'd ever seen. It was made of pure gold. Fred held the precious egg up to the light.

"Real gold!" he screamed. "We're rich!"

He ran into the house to show his wife, Tillie. She held the golden egg, turning it around and around in her fingers.

"We're no longer poor!" cried Tillie.

The next morning, they went together to gather goose eggs. Holding their straw baskets, they piled in eggs from every goose except the plain gray one. They saved her for last. Finally, when they could stand it no longer, they tiptoed to the gray goose. Fred picked up the bird while Tillie closed her eyes and reached into the nest.

"Another one!" screamed Fred, taking a new golden egg from Tillie's shaking hand.

The next day and the next, Fred and Tillie ran straight to the gray goose. And each day, the bird did not disappoint them.

When the moon came out that night, Fred lay in bed thinking.

"You know, Tillie," he said, "why should we wait for each golden egg one by one? Why don't I cut the goose open and take all the eggs at once? Then we'll be rich for life."

And that is exactly what he did. But Fred had made a terrible mistake, for when he cut the goose open, he found no eggs at all. Now the goose that laid the golden eggs was dead, along with the farmer's hopes of being rich for life.

Fred wished someone had told him that:

If You Are Greedy, You May End up with Nothing.

The Grasshopper and the Ant

Early on a frosty fall morning, Ant arranged her stores of grain for the long, cold winter ahead. She was tidying neat piles of wheat, oats, and corn when Grasshopper happened to pass by her open door. Grasshopper peered in, amazed at Ant's full pantry.

"Please, Miss," began Grasshopper politely. "Could you spare a few kernels of grain?"

Now Ant looked up from her work and stared hard at Grasshopper.

"And what were you doing during harvest while I worked from dawn to dusk collecting food for the winter?" she finally asked.

"That, my friend, is easy to explain," answered Grasshopper. "I was singing sweet songs of summer, of course. Perhaps you heard my lovely chirping."

"Yes, indeed, I did," answered Ant. "And did you enjoy yourself as you chirped away the seasons?"

"Well, yes, as a matter of fact, I did," answered Grasshopper, feeling the chill of a fall wind.

"Then surely you will understand what I must say to you now, sir," began Ant.

Grasshopper nervously rubbed his legs together.

"Since you sang all summer while I was planning for the freezing months ahead, it looks as if you will have to dance all winter just to catch up."

With this, Ant slammed tight her pantry door and disappeared into her stores of grain.

All next winter, Grasshopper will wish he'd remembered two important words:

Plan Ahead.

34

The Hare and the Tortoise

Hare enjoyed bragging about himself.

"Surely, I'm the quickest one around," he boasted to the other animals. "Of course, we all know Tortoise is the slowest."

Tortoise had heard this speech many times and was more than a little tired of it.

"But you've never proved yourself, Hare," said Tortoise. "I'll challenge you to a race. Then we'll see who is quicker."

"You're the slowest one around," laughed Hare. "But if you're serious about this silly race, fine with me."

"I may be slow, but I'm always steady," whispered Tortoise.

The animals set the racing course to start on the dirt road and end at the tall oak tree on the hill. Hare laughed as he ran circles around Tortoise at the starting line.

When Fox barked "GO," Hare sprinted down the road, leaving Tortoise in the dust. Tortoise started at once. He inched ahead at his top speed, which was very slow indeed.

Down the road, Hare looked back.

"Look at Tortoise! He's barely creeping forward!" laughed Hare. "No use wearing myself out. I'll just rest a bit before I rush ahead to the finish line."

Hare lay down under an old elm tree. But soon he grew drowsy and fell asleep, snoring loudly.

Meanwhile, Tortoise trudged forward. Little by little, he crawled through the course, until he passed sleeping Hare.

Hare awoke with a jump and saw Tortoise near the tall oak tree. He raced ahead as fast as he could, but it was too late. Tortoise had won the race!

At the finish line, Tortoise reminded Hare that:

Slow and Steady Wins the Race.

The Lion and the Fox

Lion was growing old and no longer had the great energy he once enjoyed. Hunting had become a terrible chore. He wore himself out just watching the other animals run away from him. But whether he hunted or not, Lion had to eat, so while deep in his cave, he devised a grand plan.

"Ohhh," he groaned loudly the next morning.

Other animals cautiously crept up to the mouth of Lion's cave to see what was the matter.

"Arghhh," he moaned again. "Won't someone come in and visit an old, sick lion?"

One by one, the animals stepped into the darkness of Lion's cave to find out what was wrong with Lion. And none of them ever came out again.

"I wish I'd tried this idea sooner," laughed Lion, chewing his lunch and smacking his lips.

Later in the afternoon, Fox wandered to Lion's den. "Ohhh," moaned Lion, seeing Fox's slim shadow. "Come in, Fox. I am not well, and a chat with you would be most amusing."

"I think not," said Fox wisely, "I can see by the footprints in the dust that you have had many visitors. And, strangely, all the tracks lead into your cave. Only when I see some tracks leading out will I pay you a visit."

Fox dashed away to enjoy the rest of his day, glad he knew enough to:

Learn from What Others Do.

The Lion and the Mouse

Lion napped, hidden in tall, golden grass after a busy day of hunting. As Lion slept, a small gray mouse scampered across his face. Lion felt nothing until Mouse's scrawny feet dashed over his nose.

"Ah choo!" sneezed Lion, scratching his nose, and capturing Mouse in the same instant.

Lion looked closely at his tiny catch and was about to pop him into his mouth like a peanut when he heard Mouse scream.

"Please let me go," begged Mouse. "You won't regret it. I'll be sure to repay your kindness."

"How absurd!" laughed Lion. "Whatever could a tiny fellow like you ever do to help a magnificent creature like me?"

"You never know when a small friend might do great things," pleaded Mouse.

Lion had his doubts. But he was tired and began once more to think of finishing his nap. So, in the end, he simply let Mouse go free.

The very next day, Lion was snared by the thick ropes of a hunter. While struggling with the cruel ropes around him, Lion was surprised to see Mouse scamper out of the forest.

"I've returned to repay your favor," said Mouse simply.

Then, bit by bit, Mouse gnawed the rope until finally it snapped, and Lion was free.

Lion had one thing to say:

"A Small Friend May Become a Great Friend."

The Milkmaid and the Bucket

Walking to market with a bucket of milk balanced neatly on her head, a milkmaid thought of her good fortune.

"How lucky I am," she said to herself. "With this bucket of creamy milk, I'll surely make enough money to buy the fattest hen at market. But I won't eat the hen. No, no. I'll feed the hen and she will lay a dozen of the biggest, whitest eggs. But I won't sell the eggs. I'll let the hen sit on them until they hatch into little yellow chicks. Then I'll feed the chicks and let them run in the fresh air until they grow and grow into the plumpest chickens. Only then will I sell them."

The milkmaid smiled, picturing her pretty chickens.

Her bucket tipped slightly as she thought of all that would soon happen, but not a drop of milk spilled out.

"Yes, I'll take those twelve fat chickens to market and get many pieces of gold for each one. Then with the gold, I'll buy the brightest, reddest dress I can find."

The milkmaid was so excited that she walked a bit faster now. A few drops of milk trickled over the side of the bucket.

"And when I wear that bright red dress," she continued, "all the boys will look at me and admire me and my dress."

She couldn't help but smile, "I'll pretend I don't notice, and I'll just toss my head like this ..."

Of course, when she tipped her head, the bucket toppled to the ground and all the milk rushed out. Now the milkmaid was left with nothing but an empty bucket and a new thought:

Don't Count Your Chickens Before They've Hatched.

The Monkey and the Cat

Monkey had built a fine fire and was eyeing some plump chestnuts that lay on the ground beside her.

"I wish I could roast these chestnuts right now!" she said. "Throwing the nuts into the fire is easy, but I always burn my paws taking them out."

She was thinking of a way to solve this problem when Cat slipped by and sat down beside her. Looking at Cat's slender paws gave her an idea.

"Good day, fine friend. What splendid paws you have!" said Monkey, throwing chestnuts into the fire.

The chestnuts crackled in the flames as Cat purred proudly.

"Pulling those chestnuts out of the fire must be a snap with your fine paws," said Monkey.

"Certainly," answered Cat, enjoying Monkey's flattery.

To prove her point, Cat reached into the flames and quickly pulled out a toasted chestnut.

"Wonderful," said Monkey, gobbling up the nut.

Cat licked her burned paw, but said nothing.

"That was fantastic, Cat," applauded Monkey. "That's just what I always tell everyone: Cat has such quick paws she can pull whole bunches of nuts out of a fire."

Cat foolishly pretended her paws didn't hurt as she pulled each and every nut out of the flames. One by one, Monkey gobbled them up until fat and full, she strolled home. Cat walked away slowly, with burning paws. Maybe next time she'll know:

It Is Foolish to Listen to Flattery.

The Porcupine
and the Snake

It was almost winter. Snake had found a perfect cave for the cold weather to come. Coiling herself up, she sighed, "This is ideal!"

Porcupine had not been so fortunate. He'd searched long and hard for a proper winter home and had found nothing. Discovering Snake's cave, he was greatly relieved.

"Finally!" he exclaimed. "I'll be warm and safe here no matter how long winter lasts!"

Suddenly, he was startled by Snake, who hissed from a shadowy corner.

"Oh, excuse me," apologized Porcupine. "I didn't mean to intrude. I had no idea this cave was already taken."

Now Porcupine looked around the dark cave. It really WAS perfect for a long winter's stay.

"Would you mind terribly, Snake, if I took just one tiny corner of your cave? It's already so chilly outside," he shivered.

"Well, I don't know you. But you look neat and clean," Snake answered. "I suppose you may stay."

Porcupine moved in immediately, curled himself up into a cozy ball, and stuck out his sharp quills.

Soon Snake realized her terrible mistake. Wherever she went, she pricked herself on pointy porcupine quills.

"This will never do!" hissed Snake. "Porcupine, I stick myself every time I move."

"Oh, how dreadful!" cried Porcupine. "Of course, you must move out. I'm sure that in no time at all you'll find a new cave that suits you much better."

Snake just learned that:

It Is Wise to Know a Guest Well
Before You Invite Him in.

The Rooster and the Jewel

Rooster pecked busily at the ground in his farmyard. He looked for choice bits of corn and oats. Around and around he pecked, searching buckets and grain bins for his favorite lunch.

Rooster had no way of knowing that just the day before the farmer had lost her diamond ring near the barn. She'd spent hours searching for this piece of jewelry, which was her wedding ring. Sad and spent, the woman had returned home empty-handed.

Now, as Rooster pecked his way around the yard, he spied something shiny near the red barn. This was, of course, the farmer's precious ring. He inched up to it and pecked it with his beak.

"That's really hard!" he exclaimed. "But it is also a challenge."

So he pecked again.

"Very hard!" exclaimed Rooster.

He tried once more.

"Much too hard," he continued. "And not a bit tasty, either," he decided.

Rooster looked at the shiny diamond ring.

"This may be a fine prize to some, but I certainly don't understand it. Just give me corn and oats, for a tasty lunch is what I appreciate."

And with that, Rooster left the diamond and forgot it forever.

Rooster proved:

It Is Impossible to Appreciate What You Don't Understand.

The Stork and the Fox

One day, Fox invited Stork over for a delicious dinner.

"How wonderful it smells!" exclaimed Stork as he entered Fox's home.

"Thank you, friend," answered Fox. "I have cooked a savory soup. Now I will serve it in my very finest china for us to share."

Stork thought this was very gracious until he saw that the soup was in a thin, flat dish. With his long, narrow beak, Stork could take no more than a few tiny sips of the delicious-smelling soup. Hungry Stork returned home, feeling Fox had not treated him quite right. But before he left, he offered Fox an invitation.

"I'd be very happy if you would come to my house tomorrow for dinner," said Stork. "Then I will make something equally delicious for us to share."

The next night when Fox arrived at Stork's home, he, too, was greeted with the warm aroma of a superb soup. But this time, it was Fox who was in for a disappointment.

"Please join me," said Stork, pointing to a tall, long-necked jar with a tiny opening at the top. "Please notice, Fox, that I am using my favorite china, too."

Stork immediately stuck his long beak into the narrow jar, but Fox could find no way to get his broad snout in. Fox went hungry this time, but perhaps it served him right, for he had forgotten a golden rule:

Treat Others as You Would Like Them to Treat You.

50

The Strong Bunch of Sticks

There were once three children who quarreled constantly. Their father felt sad that his children did not get along with one another.

"Come here," said the father softly.

The three children sheepishly approached their father, for they were afraid he would punish them for fighting. The father sensed their fear.

"I will not punish you," he explained. "But I WILL open your eyes."

Then the man showed them a bunch of sticks he had tied tightly together.

"Take this bunch of sticks and break it in two," commanded the father.

The children looked at each other, not understanding. But each one took a turn and tried to break the bunch of sticks.

"It is impossible. They are too strong to break," said the oldest after all three had tried.

The father shook his head, understanding. Then he untied the bunch of sticks and gave just one to each child.

"Now break the sticks," he said.

Alone, each stick broke easily. And now the father explained:

"You have just learned an important lesson. If you work together like the bunch of sticks, you will be strong. But when you fight, each for yourself, you are weak, and can easily be broken."

Now the children hugged their father, for with only a bunch of sticks he had taught them:

People Are Strong When They Work Together.

The Turtle and the Eagle

Turtle crawled slowly through the sand one breezy afternoon. Looking up, he spied eagles flying high in the sky. "How they soar and dive!" thought Turtle. "I don't want to crawl in the sand forever. I want to fly with the birds."

"Eagle," he shouted to a gliding bird. "Please, friend, teach me to fly."

"You're not built for flying," laughed Eagle. "Your shell is heavy, and you have no wings or feathers."

"But with a fine teacher like you, perhaps it is possible," pleaded Turtle.

"Your body is perfect for crawling through the sand," said Eagle. "Be satisfied with that."

But Turtle shook his head and begged, "If you teach me to fly, I'll bring you shiny treasures from the sea."

"Well, if you insist, perhaps it's worth a try," answered Eagle, with dark, sparkling eyes.

Eagle lifted Turtle with his sharp talons. Gliding high over rocky cliffs, Turtle looked down on the sand far below.

"Flying is wonderful," hummed Turtle.

"Now it is time to begin the lesson," squawked Eagle.

With those words, Eagle released his powerful talons. Turtle flapped his flippers as quickly as he could. But he fell through the air until he crashed into the sharp rocks beside the sea. That was the end of the flying lesson. And that was the end of Turtle.

If Turtle could tell you what he thought of all this, he would say:

"Be Satisfied with Who You Are."

The Two Frogs

Right in the middle of a hot summer, a vast lake dried up. Two frogs, who had made their home at the lake, realized it was time to move on. They hopped all over the countryside, searching for water until they came to a deep stone well.

"Perhaps there is water in the well," said the first frog.

"Yes," said the second frog. "Let's throw in a stone. If we hear a splash, we will know the old well still has water."

The first frog found a big stone. Then together the two frogs carried it to the top of the well and threw it down.

It took a few moments for the stone to hit bottom, but when it did, there was a loud splash.

"Water!" the two frogs yelled happily together.

"Let's leap in," said the first frog, ready to jump.

But the second frog held back her friend.

"Wait," she explained. "It took a long time for the stone to hit the water."

"Yes?" asked her friend, not understanding.

"If we jump into the well, we may find the water," said the second frog. "But it may take a good long time before we ever get out."

The first frog thought about this while the two friends moved on to find water in a safer place.

Maybe the story of the two frogs will remind you to:

Look Before You Leap.

The Wasps in the Honey Pot

Three wasps landed on a sweet treasure one sticky summer afternoon, for someone had left an open honey pot outside on a garden table. Drips of sweet honey oozed over the brim of the tall pot onto the table. Sampling the honey that had dribbled out, the wasps found it was excellent.

"This is surely our lucky day!" said the first wasp.

With that, the three wasps jumped right into the honey pot and started eating.

"Perhaps we should save some honey for tomorrow," suggested the second wasp.

"That would be most foolish," laughed the third wasp. "For all we know, the person who left this wonderful honey will come back. That would be the end of it for us."

"Yes," agreed the first wasp. "This could be our last chance for such a fine meal."

So the wasps ate and ate and ate. And as the honey disappeared, the wasps grew fatter and fatter and fatter. Before they knew it, they were at the bottom of the honey pot.

"I think it's time to go," groaned the first wasp, heavy with honey.

But the pot was sticky, and the wasps were full. No matter how hard they tried, they couldn't crawl, walk, or fly out of that pot. So there they stayed, thinking:

Too Much of a Good Thing Is Too Much.

The Wind and the Sun

Wind and Sun were arguing about who was stronger.

"I am surely stronger," boasted Wind. "I am able to blow autumn leaves off the trees. I can power the largest sailboats and turn the heaviest windmills with just a single breeze."

"Since you are so sure of yourself," suggested Sun, "we should have a contest."

"Fine," said Wind. "The one who can make a traveler take off his coat will win the contest."

"That sounds fair to me," agreed Sun. "Here comes a traveler. You try first."

As Sun hid behind the clouds, Wind took a deep breath and blew wildly.

Instantly, the traveler pulled his coat around his body. The gale grew harsher until the man walked with his eyes closed tightly against the blustering wind. His face was pinched with pain, but the traveler held tightly to his coat, and did not take it off.

"It's impossible," gasped Wind. "But go ahead and try."

"With pleasure," said Sun, coming out from behind the clouds.

Now Sun beat gently on the traveler with bright, warm rays. The traveler smiled up at the sky, did a happy little dance in the middle of his walk, and then took off his heavy coat.

Sun didn't have to say another word to Wind, who finally saw that:

Being Gentle Often Works Better than Being Harsh.

The Wolf in Sheep's Clothing

Wolf was tired of hunting, but felt hungry for a big dinner. Finding an old sheepskin in the woods, he designed a clever plan.

"I will disguise myself and pretend I am one of the sheep!" Wolf said, amazed at his own craftiness. "Then I'll join the flock, take my time, pounce upon a tasty lamb, and enjoy my dinner."

He neatly tied the sheepskin around himself, and after a few tucks here and there, was sure that he looked just like one of the sheep. Then he slowly walked into the meadow and began to nibble on the grass. Some of the sheep looked at him strangely, but couldn't figure out what was different about this new member of the flock.

At the end of the day, Wolf was delighted when he was locked up with the sheep.

"Now I will grab the fattest sheep and eat it for dinner," said Wolf, already smacking his lips. "Which one shall I choose?"

At that moment, the shepherd opened the gate.

"Which one shall I choose?" asked the shepherd, looking over the flock. "That one is surely bigger than all the rest," he said, pointing to Wolf. "So he will be my dinner."

In an instant, the shepherd took out his knife and killed the sheep who wasn't a sheep at all. The shepherd was shocked to find Wolf hiding under the old sheepskin. But, of course, Wolf had been even more shocked. He'd had no time to learn that:

Pretending to Be Something You Aren't Can Be Very Dangerous.

The Woman and the Fat Hen

A woman had an old hen that laid one big white egg every day just in time for her breakfast. One morning when the woman went to fetch her breakfast egg, she was delighted to find there were two.

"How could it have happened?" asked the woman. "I do believe I fed the hen an extra bit of corn yesterday. Yes, that must be it!"

All day the woman thought about her old hen and how wonderful it would be to eat two eggs every morning.

"I know just what to do!" said the woman. "I will feed her even more corn. Then maybe she'll give me two eggs every morning."

The woman kept thinking, and her thoughts were very greedy indeed.

"If I feed her more corn, and also add some oats and barley, maybe she'll give me three eggs," she said hopefully.

So the woman began to feed more and more corn, oats, and barley to her old hen. The hen was happy to cooperate, and soon became the fattest in the county.

But the woman's plan failed miserably, for the old hen grew so very fat that it stopped laying eggs altogether. The woman missed her one egg in the morning, and quickly put her hen on a strict diet. Each morning when she checked to see if the hen had begun to lay eggs again, the woman thought:

One Who Is Greedy May End up with Less Instead of More.

About Aesop

Aesop was a Greek slave and gifted storyteller who lived more than 2,500 years ago. He collected fables that had been told for hundreds of years. Although he never wrote them down, he retold them in very clever ways. Aesop told his stories so well that the king eventually freed him to reward his great talent.

Most of Aesop's stories are about animals who learn important lessons, or morals, through wise or foolish acts. By using animals, Aesop could safely point out people's mistakes and weaknesses. The stories gently poke fun while giving us a clear look at human nature.

For many years, Aesop was very popular, and traveled far and wide with his stories. But not everyone admired the storyteller. Some felt the "teaching tales" insulted them. One day in Delphi, people grew so angry with Aesop and his fables that they pushed him off a cliff. The storyteller plunged to his death.

Today people throughout the world read Aesop's fables. Because they give us such a good look at human nature, it is not surprising that they have survived for thousands of years. Most likely, they will last for thousands more.

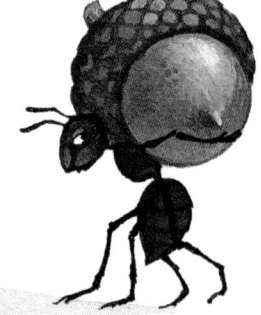